Many thanks to the cover colorist, Shelly Pfeiffer, who made this book look extra colorful!

This book is dedicated to my friend and online assistant, Jessica Johnson. You see my sass and raise it with snark and I love you for that. You're there for me day or night even while managing your own businesses and ventures. Whether I need your computer knowledge, an administrative task completed, marketing ideas, or just a silly late-night chat, you're always there for me and make me feel like a rock star. Thank you for always listening to my rants, reminding me who I am, and for being my sounding board. I love you, girl!

xoxo, Mama Sass

Much love to my coloring team who give me feedback, suggestions, ideas, and work to help promote my work: Jessica Johnson, Jennifer Scarabin, Lisa Frey, Rachel Gillham, Kelly Taylor, Jennifer Vinson, Kim Fulmer, Kristin Russo, Lina Weikel, Katie Hoffman, Michelle Huntley-Herrema, Molly Wee, Megan Page, Shelly Pfeiffer, Elizabeth Herriot, Gayla Albert, Domineek Bumpas, Natalie Jo Barnes Chacon, and Dawn Meredith.

If you like this book, please leave a review on Amazon!

MENOPAUSAL MANIA & MAYHEM

AN ADULT COLORING BOOK OF HORMONAL HERESY

CRISTIN APRIL FREY

COLORIST: _____DATE COMPLETED: _____

MEDIUM USED: _____

COLORIST: _____ DATE COMPLETED: _____

MEDIUM USED: _____

WELCOME to menopause

(you'll need these)

CristinApril.com

COLORIST: _____DATE COMPLETED: _____

MEDIUM USED: _____

COLORIST: _____ DATE COMPLETED: _____

MEDIUM USED: _____

MENOPAUSE MAKES ME TEMPERMENTAL

HALF TEMPER HALF MENTAL

MENOPAUSAL MANIA & MAYHEM: AN ADULT COLORING BOOK OF HORMONAL HERESY

COLORIST: _____ DATE COMPLETED: _____

MEDIUM USED: _____

BRAIN FOG

DIZZINESS

HAIR LOSS

LIBIDO

FACIAL HAIR

Menopause is NO place for sissies.

fatigue

weight gain

SORE BOOBS

HOT FLASHES

night sweats

insomnia

MENOPAUSAL MANIA & MAYHEM: AN ADULT COLORING BOOK OF HORMONAL HERESY

COLORIST: _____ DATE COMPLETED: _____

MEDIUM USED: _____

©CristinApril.com

COLORIST: _____DATE COMPLETED: _____

MEDIUM USED: _____

The older you get, the more dangerous it is to sneeze.

©CristinApril.com

MENOPAUSAL MANIA & MAYHEM: AN ADULT COLORING BOOK OF HORMONAL HERESY

COLORIST: _____DATE COMPLETED: _____

MEDIUM USED: _____

just
laugh
until you leak

©CristinApril.com

COLORIST: _____DATE COMPLETED: _____

MEDIUM USED: _____

©CristinApril.com

MENOPAUSAL MANIA & MAYHEM: AN ADULT COLORING BOOK OF HORMONAL HERESY

COLORIST: _____ DATE COMPLETED: _____

MEDIUM USED: _____

I PUT THE HOT IN IDAHO

MENOPAUSAL MANIA & MAYHEM: AN ADULT COLORING BOOK OF HORMONAL HERESY

COLORIST: _____ DATE COMPLETED: _____

MEDIUM USED: _____

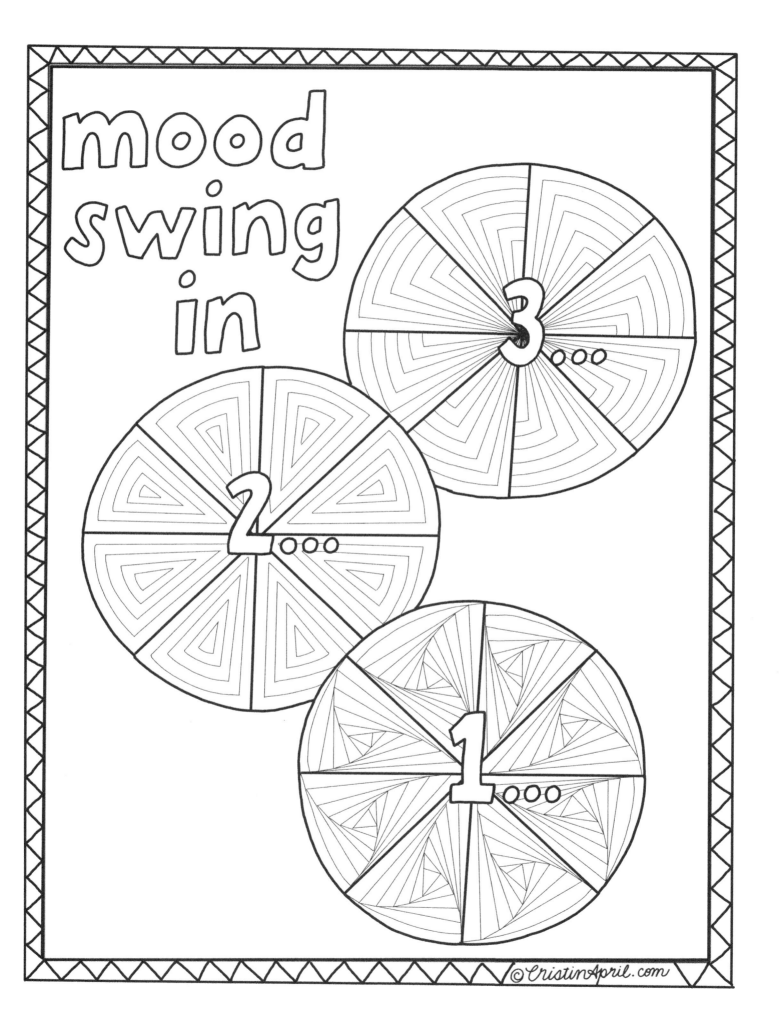

COLORIST: _____DATE COMPLETED: _____

MEDIUM USED: _____

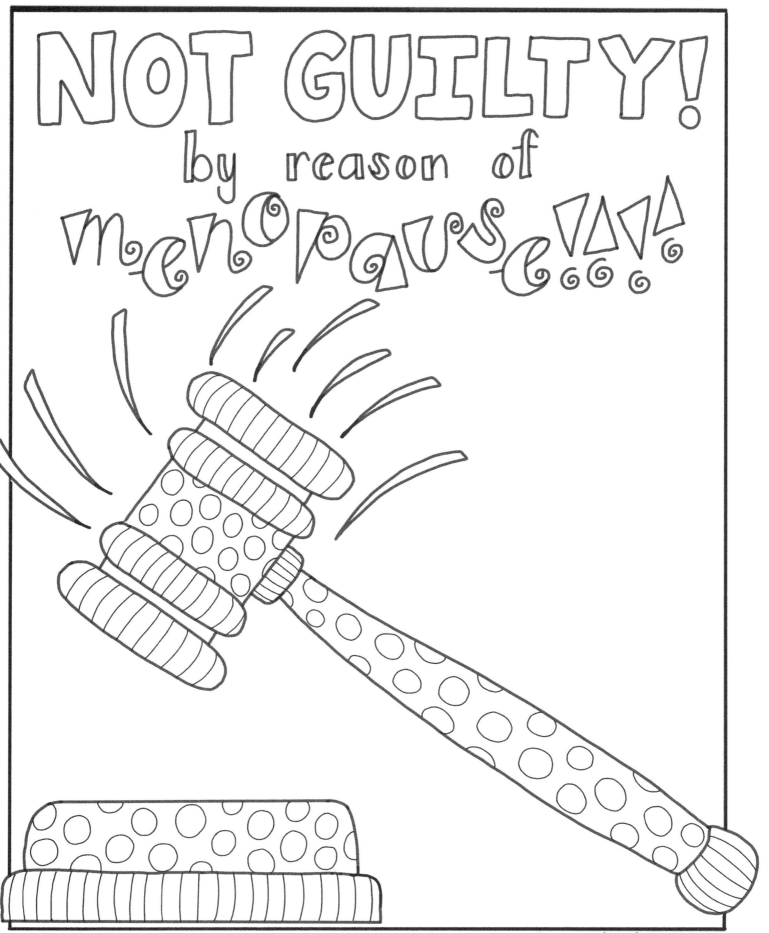

©CristinApril.com

I HAVE TWO SETTINGS:

ETERNAL HELLFIRE

or

HYPOTHERMIA

MENOPAUSAL MANIA & MAYHEM: AN ADULT COLORING BOOK OF HORMONAL HERESY

COLORIST: _____DATE COMPLETED: _____

MEDIUM USED: _____

HORMONAL OR NOT IONAL

©CristinApril.com

Mirror, mirror, on the wall, what the hell happened?

COLORIST: _____DATE COMPLETED: _____

MEDIUM USED: _____

Bonus Pages

10 menopausal mandalas

COLORIST: _____ DATE COMPLETED: _____

MEDIUM USED: _____

COLORIST: _____DATE COMPLETED: _____

MEDIUM USED: _____

MOPEY

COLORIST: _____DATE COMPLETED: _____

MEDIUM USED: _____

MENOPAUSAL MANIA & MAYHEM: AN ADULT COLORING BOOK OF HORMONAL HERESY

COLORIST: _____DATE COMPLETED: _____

MEDIUM USED: _____

CristinApril.com

COLORIST: _____DATE COMPLETED: _____

MEDIUM USED: _____

©CristinApril.com

CristinApril.com

COLORIST: _____DATE COMPLETED: _____

MEDIUM USED: _____

©CristinApril.com

COLORIST: _____ DATE COMPLETED: _____

MEDIUM USED: _____

COLOR TESTING PAGE

USE THIS PAGE TO TEST YOUR COLORS. CREATE COLOR SCHEMES. KEEP TRACK OF THE COLORS YOU USE. OR PRACTICE BLENDING.

COLOR TESTING PAGE

USE THIS PAGE TO TEST YOUR COLORS. CREATE COLOR SCHEMES. KEEP TRACK OF THE COLORS YOU USE. OR PRACTICE BLENDING.

COLOR TESTING PAGE

USE THIS PAGE TO TEST YOUR COLORS. CREATE COLOR SCHEMES. KEEP TRACK OF THE COLORS YOU USE. OR PRACTICE BLENDING.

About the Artist: Cristin is a self-taught artist who loves doodling, lettering, and sarcasm. She has combined these things into hand-drawn, original coloring pages for others to enjoy. Cristin resides in upstate New York with her rescue dogs, her rescue husband, her daughter, and lots of coffee and wine.

Cristin loves seeing your colored pages and wants you to show her!

Facebook: www.facebook.com/cristinaprilsart

Twitter: www.twitter.com/cristinapril

Instagram: www.instagram.com/cristinapril

Pinterest: www.pinterest.com/cristinapril

#CRISTINAPRILSART

If you enjoyed this book, please leave a review on Amazon.com!

Visit www.CristinApril.com to sign up for the free Colorholics Anonymous Club!

You will receive free monthly coloring pages, coupon codes, coloring tips and tricks, the newest updates, and much more!

Other books from Cristin April Frey:

Sassy Sayings, Snarky Sarcasms, & Saucy Swears

The Art of Not Giving a F*ck: A Callous Adult Coloring Book of Disregard

(Available on Amazon.com)

Digital versions and individual pages available to download at CristinApril.com.